Embroidery: Principles of Design

Cambridge University Press
CAMBRIDGE
LONDON   NEW YORK   MELBOURNE

BY LILLIAN ROGERS

Introduction to Embroidery   *Embroidery: Looking for Ideas*
Embroidery: Working Stitches   *Embroidery: Principles of Design*

This series of books is designed to present the first essentials of Embroidery in a visual form. Each stage is illustrated by a drawing and careful explanation so that beginners can develop their skills stage by stage. The ideas this Series of books provide can be developed by individuals in a way that depends on their own particular skills and interests.

People using this Series of books as a preparation for examinations can mount samples of their work on coloured sheets of paper as worksheets for the purpose of assessment. When users have worked through the complete Series they will have a number of worksheets to show as an indication of the kind of work they can achieve.

Embroidery: Principles of Design shows how such varied subjects as letters, buildings, birds and kitchens can be used as inspiration for embroidery design. Various techniques are demonstrated: several different types of quilting, blackwork, mounting embroidery, covering lampshades, making cords and fringes; and many ideas for three-dimensional embroidery are also presented.

Contents

Lettering as a source of inspiration   2
Blackwork   5
Quilting   6
Buildings as a source of inspiration   12
Three-dimensional embroidery   16
Desert and cactus collage   20
Mounting of work for framing   23
The kitchen as a source of inspiration   24
Lampshade in shadow-work   26
Cords and fringes   29
Bird collage   30

Published by the Syndics of the Cambridge University Press
The Pitt Building, Trumpington Street, Cambridge CB2 1RP
Bentley House, 200 Euston Road, London NW1 2DB
32 East 57th Street, New York, NY 10022, USA
296 Beaconsfield Parade, Middle Park, Melbourne 3206, Australia

First published 1980

Printed in Great Britain by
David Green (Printers) Ltd, Kettering, Northamptonshire

ISBN 0 521 21556 0

Lettering as a source of inspiration

First draw each letter carefully, in plain block shape. Trace this letter and add the decorative shaping.

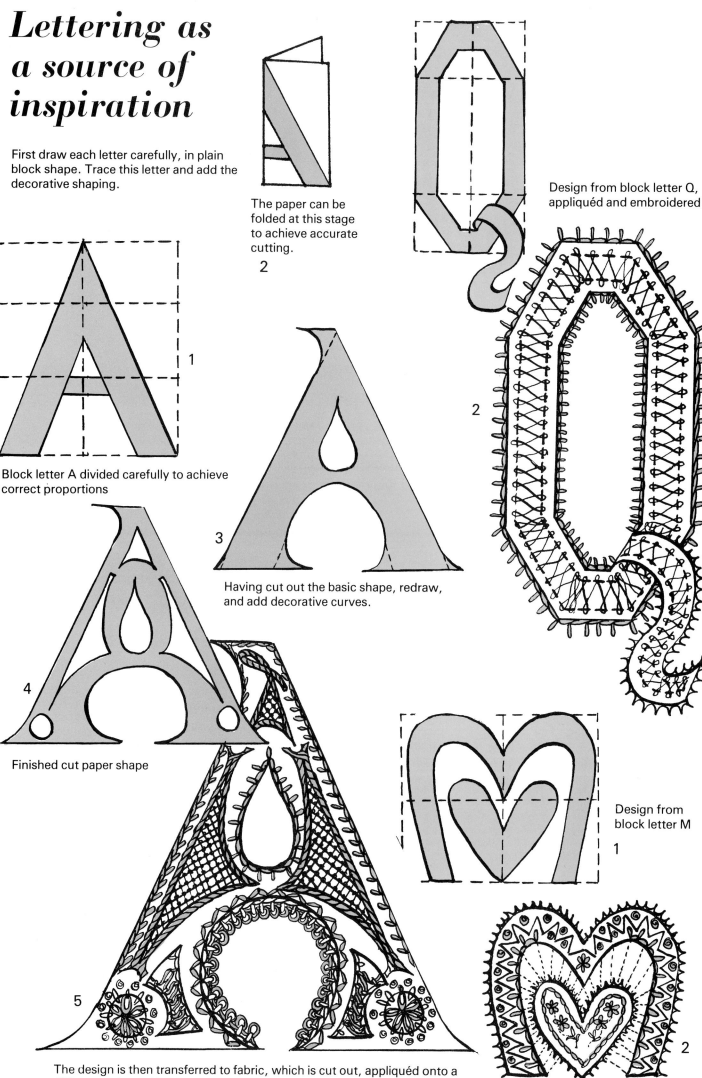

The paper can be folded at this stage to achieve accurate cutting.
2

Design from block letter Q, appliquéd and embroidered

2

Block letter A divided carefully to achieve correct proportions
1

3

Having cut out the basic shape, redraw, and add decorative curves.

4

Finished cut paper shape

Design from block letter M
1

5

The design is then transferred to fabric, which is cut out, appliquéd onto a different-coloured background and embroidered.

2

2

Unusual ways of using letters

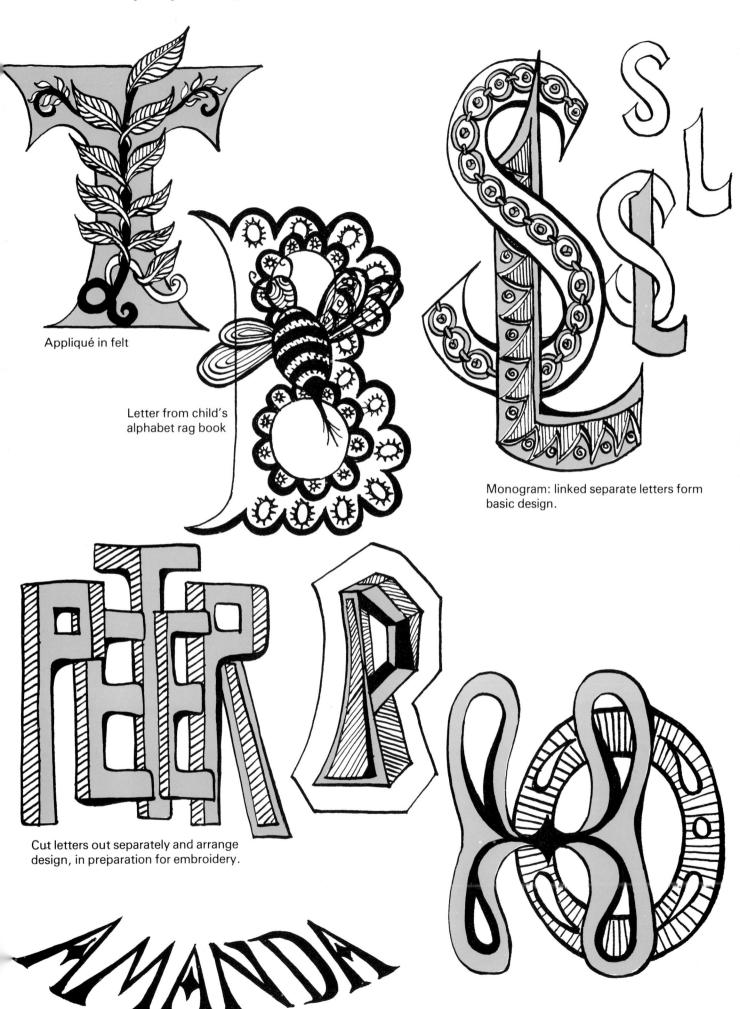

Appliqué in felt

Letter from child's alphabet rag book

Monogram: linked separate letters form basic design.

Cut letters out separately and arrange design, in preparation for embroidery.

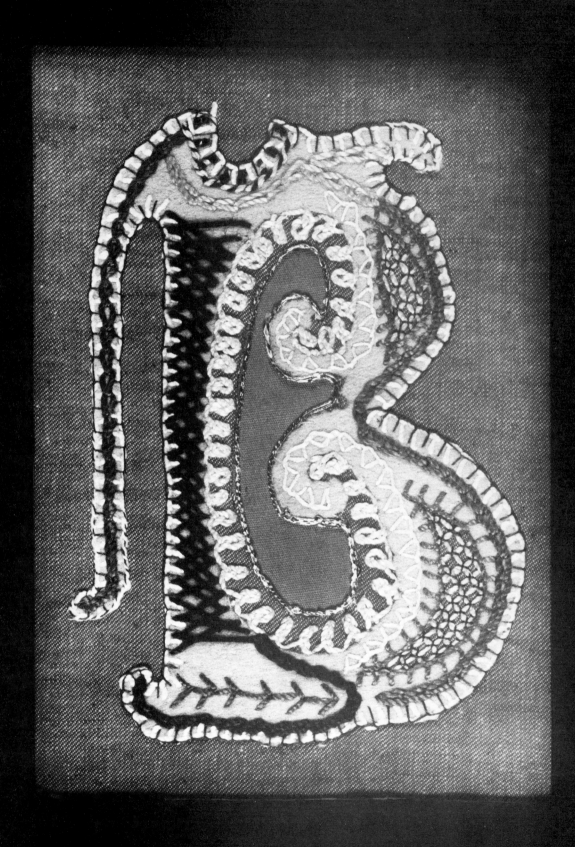

Blackwork

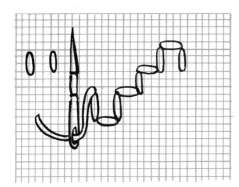

Holbein stitch: a straight stitch over counted threads, outlining shape; then a linking stitch back

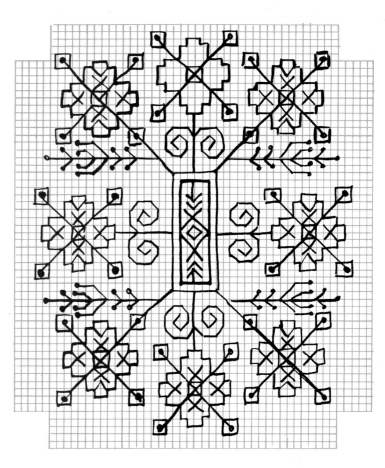

Blackwork originated during the sixteenth century, and is black stitching on a white or cream background, generally over counted threads. The shapes are geometrical, and executed in either a single strand, or thicker Coton à Broder to give a varied texture. Designs should be worked out on graph paper first.

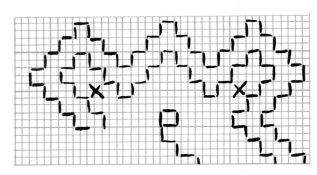

Border pattern in Holbein stitch

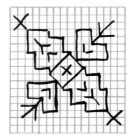

Motifs

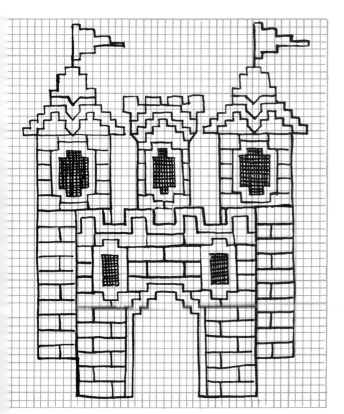

Castle design worked in Holbein stitch, windows in laid work

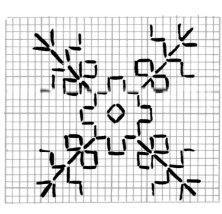

Quilting *English quilting*

Quilting originated as a method of keeping warm, but soon developed into a highly decorative skill, used for clothing, curtains, cushions, etc. The English variety is distinguished by the use of three layers of fabric: a top layer of satin, brocade or firm cotton, a central layer of wadding or flannel, and a thin cotton backing. The work is stitched through the three layers.

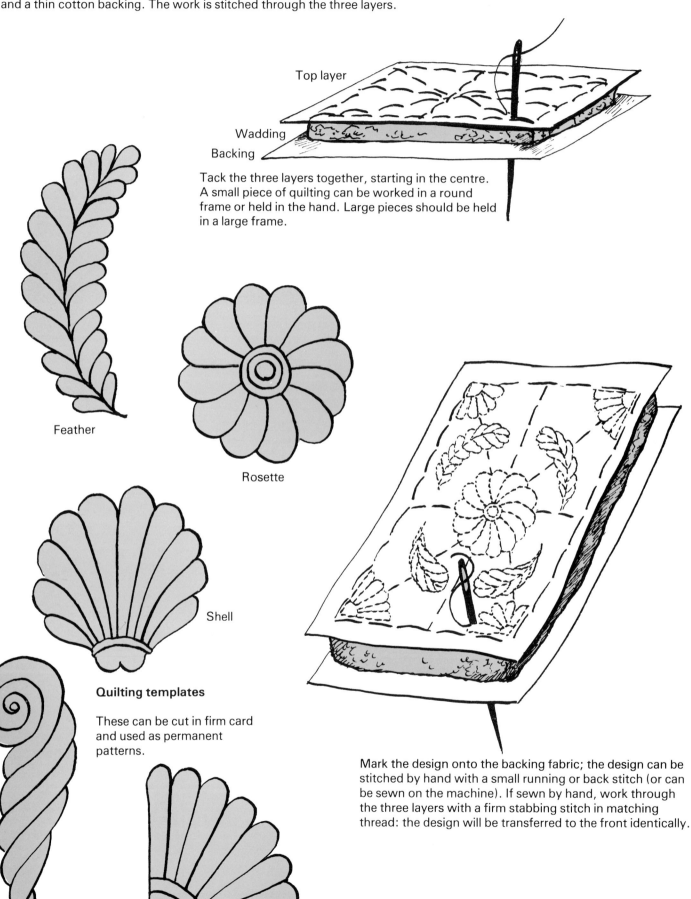

Top layer

Wadding

Backing

Tack the three layers together, starting in the centre. A small piece of quilting can be worked in a round frame or held in the hand. Large pieces should be held in a large frame.

Feather

Rosette

Shell

Quilting templates

These can be cut in firm card and used as permanent patterns.

Fan

Mark the design onto the backing fabric; the design can be stitched by hand with a small running or back stitch (or can be sewn on the machine). If sewn by hand, work through the three layers with a firm stabbing stitch in matching thread: the design will be transferred to the front identically.

Articles using English quilting, in traditional designs

Cot quilt in cotton satin padded with Terylene wadding: rosette, fan and rabbit design

Bag in firm cotton fabric with cane handle: fan and rosette design

Roll pillow in satin with gathered end pieces and tassels: feather design

Waistcoat in heavy satin with bound edges: feather and clamshell design

Jewellery box in satin: rosette and clamshell design

Italian quilting

Italian quilting differs from English quilting in that only two layers of fabric are used. An enclosed shape is sewn either by hand or machine, and a cord is drawn through the channel between the stitches, from the wrong side.

The two layers of fabric are tacked together. The design is then sewn either by hand or machine, leaving clear channels.

The design is traced with wheel and carbon onto backing fabric.

Finished appearance of Italian quilting

This method of quilting can be used on many types of fabric, including leather. The raised surface is very attractive, but is not used on an article primarily for warmth.

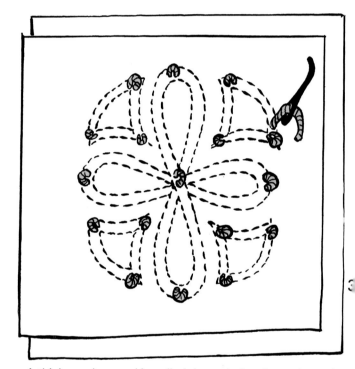

A thick wool or cord is pulled through the channels on the back layer.

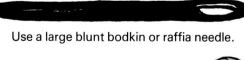

Use a large blunt bodkin or raffia needle.

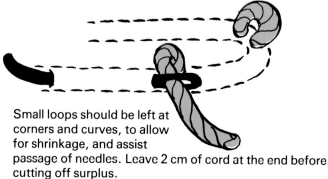

Small loops should be left at corners and curves, to allow for shrinkage, and assist passage of needles. Leave 2 cm of cord at the end before cutting off surplus.

Articles in Italian quilting

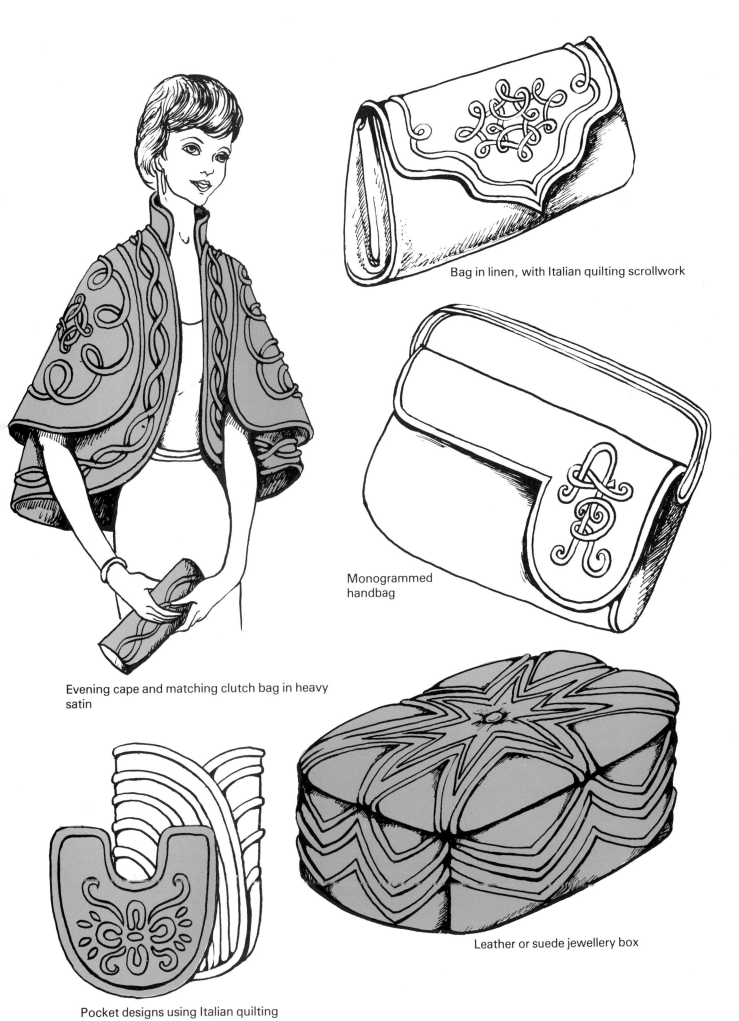

Bag in linen, with Italian quilting scrollwork

Monogrammed handbag

Evening cape and matching clutch bag in heavy satin

Leather or suede jewellery box

Pocket designs using Italian quilting

Other forms of quilting

Suffolk puffs

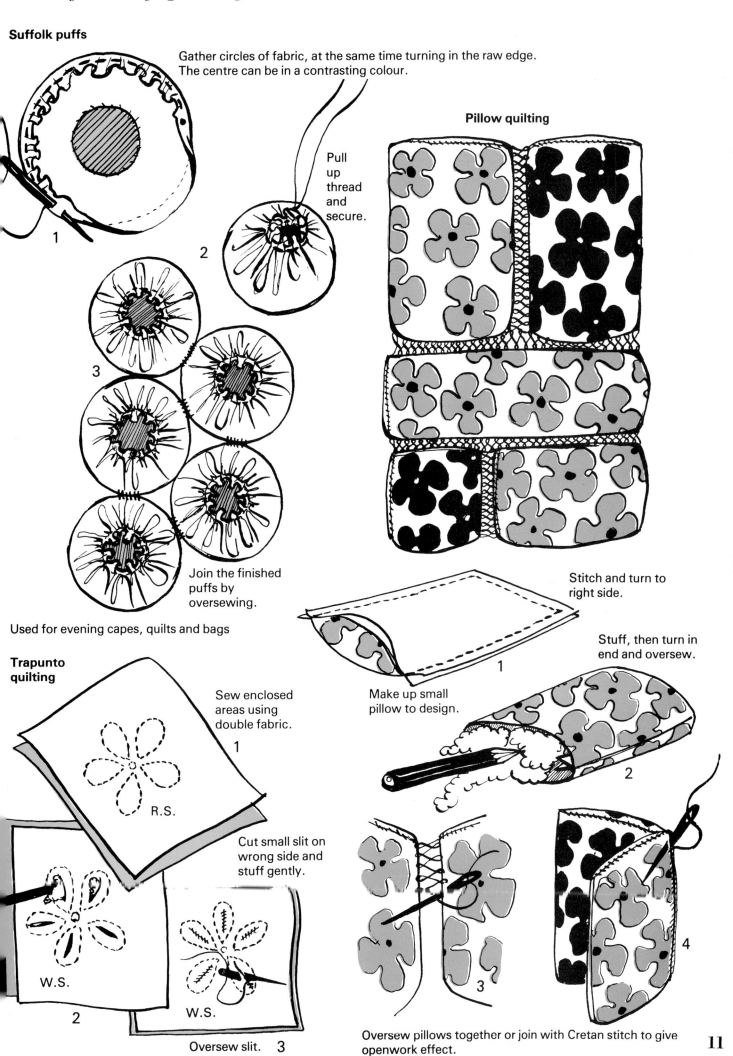

Gather circles of fabric, at the same time turning in the raw edge. The centre can be in a contrasting colour.

1

Pull up thread and secure.

2

3

Join the finished puffs by oversewing.

Used for evening capes, quilts and bags

Pillow quilting

Stitch and turn to right side.

Make up small pillow to design.

1

Stuff, then turn in end and oversew.

2

Trapunto quilting

Sew enclosed areas using double fabric.

1

R.S.

Cut small slit on wrong side and stuff gently.

W.S.

2

W.S.

Oversew slit.   3

3

4

Oversew pillows together or join with Cretan stitch to give openwork effect.

Made by pupil of Woodberry Down
School, aged 15 years

Buildings as a source of inspiration

Buildings can be used on their own, or incorporated in a street collage.
A scrapbook of photographs and sketches is very useful.

Street drawing 1

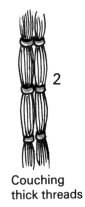

2

Couching
thick threads

Adaptation of street scene, abstract design,
using appliqué and couching

Openwork wheel

Alternating
blanket stitch

Satin stitch

Couching

2

Design from a Tudor house, interpreted in
blackwork and surface stitchery on even-weave
fabric

Pen drawing of Tudor house, either from life or
traced from a photograph

13

Buildings as a source of inspiration

Industrial scenery 1

Water and radio towers

Design of industrial scene, translated into embroidery 2

Abstracted design from Post Office Tower

2

Drawing of Brighton Pavilion 1

Dome of Brighton Pavilion, worked in appliqué and cording

Buildings as a source of inspiration

Pen drawings of street scene

1

Drawing interpreted in embroidery

2

Laid work for woodwork

Looped blanket stitch for roof

Brickwork in blanket stitch

Board in satin stitch

Black raffia for windows

Aerials in backstitch

This design can be worked in either black and white or colour.

16

Three-dimensional embroidery

String can be used to add texture to embroidery, in macramé, or as a combination of both to give decorative and unusual effects. Used with adhesive, a variety of textures can be obtained. (Use a rubber-based solution such as Copydex or P.V.C.)

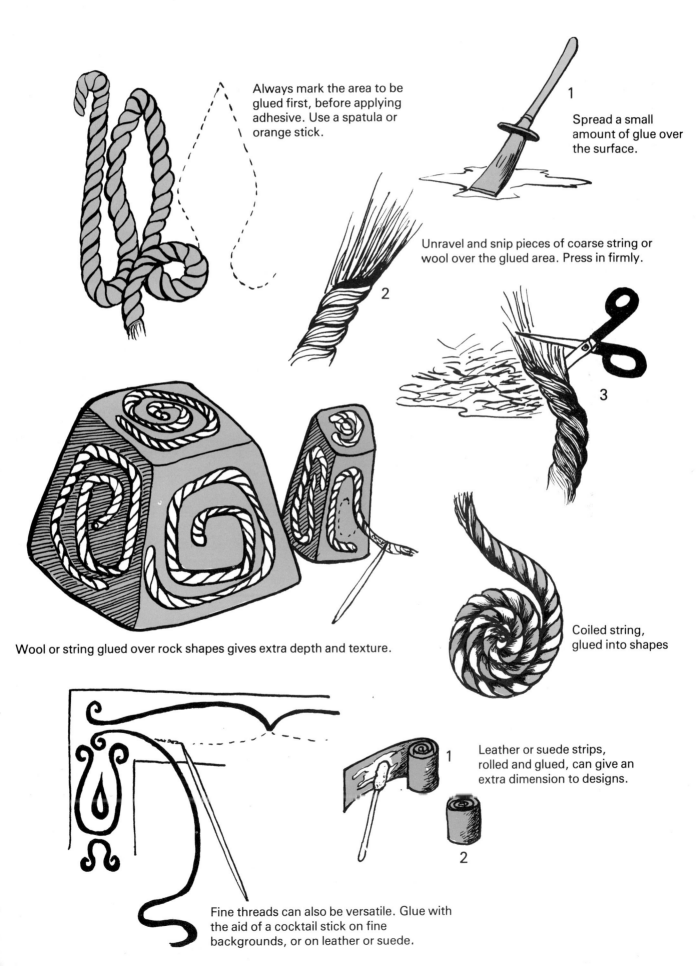

Always mark the area to be glued first, before applying adhesive. Use a spatula or orange stick.

1 Spread a small amount of glue over the surface.

Unravel and snip pieces of coarse string or wool over the glued area. Press in firmly.

2

3

Wool or string glued over rock shapes gives extra depth and texture.

Coiled string, glued into shapes

Leather or suede strips, rolled and glued, can give an extra dimension to designs.

1

2

Fine threads can also be versatile. Glue with the aid of a cocktail stick on fine backgrounds, or on leather or suede.

Three-dimensional embroidery

Use three-dimensional embroidery to build up surfaces on a collage. The medium can be varied to suit the background. Many methods can be used, such as cardboard shapes covered with wool or silk, layers of felt or leather, beads and canvas work.

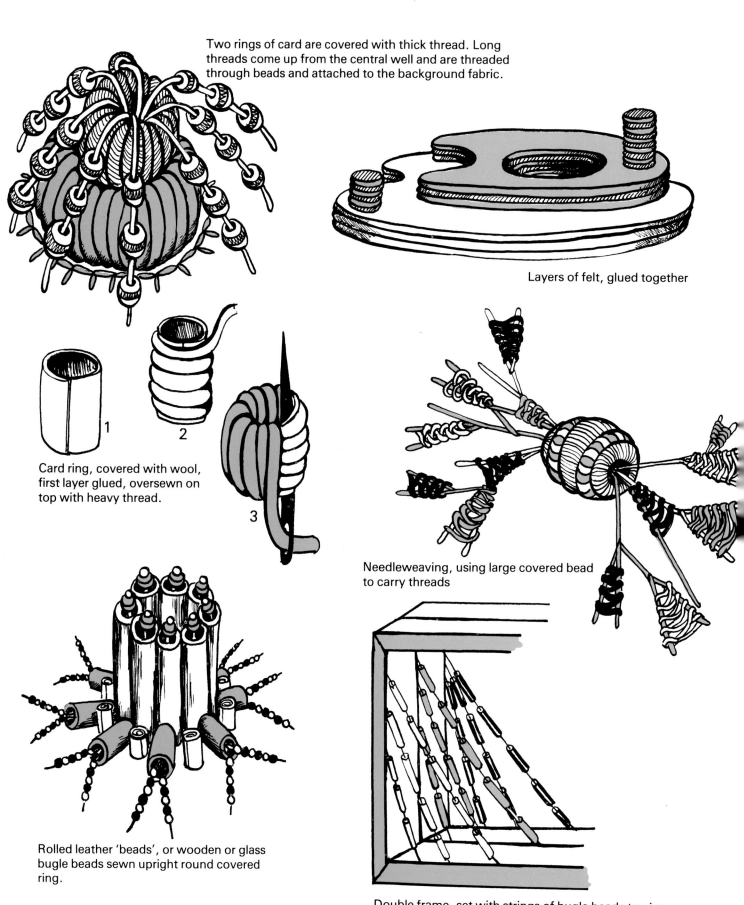

Two rings of card are covered with thick thread. Long threads come up from the central well and are threaded through beads and attached to the background fabric.

Layers of felt, glued together

Card ring, covered with wool, first layer glued, oversewn on top with heavy thread.

Needleweaving, using large covered bead to carry threads

Rolled leather 'beads', or wooden or glass bugle beads sewn upright round covered ring.

Double frame, set with strings of bugle beads to give a three-dimensional effect

Desert and cactus collage

Square off design. Enlarge to required size.
Measure the separate areas to give some
indication of the amount of fabric needed for
each cactus.

1

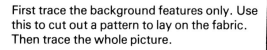

First trace the background features only. Use
this to cut out a pattern to lay on the fabric.
Then trace the whole picture.

2

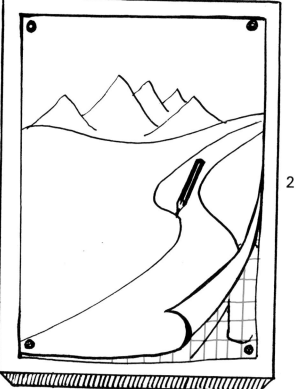

3

Place dressmaker's carbon face down on the
right side of the fabric. Pin the whole tracing
over this and, with a tracing wheel, mark the
position of the main features. The tracing can
then be cut out and used for the pattern pieces.

Desert and cactus collage

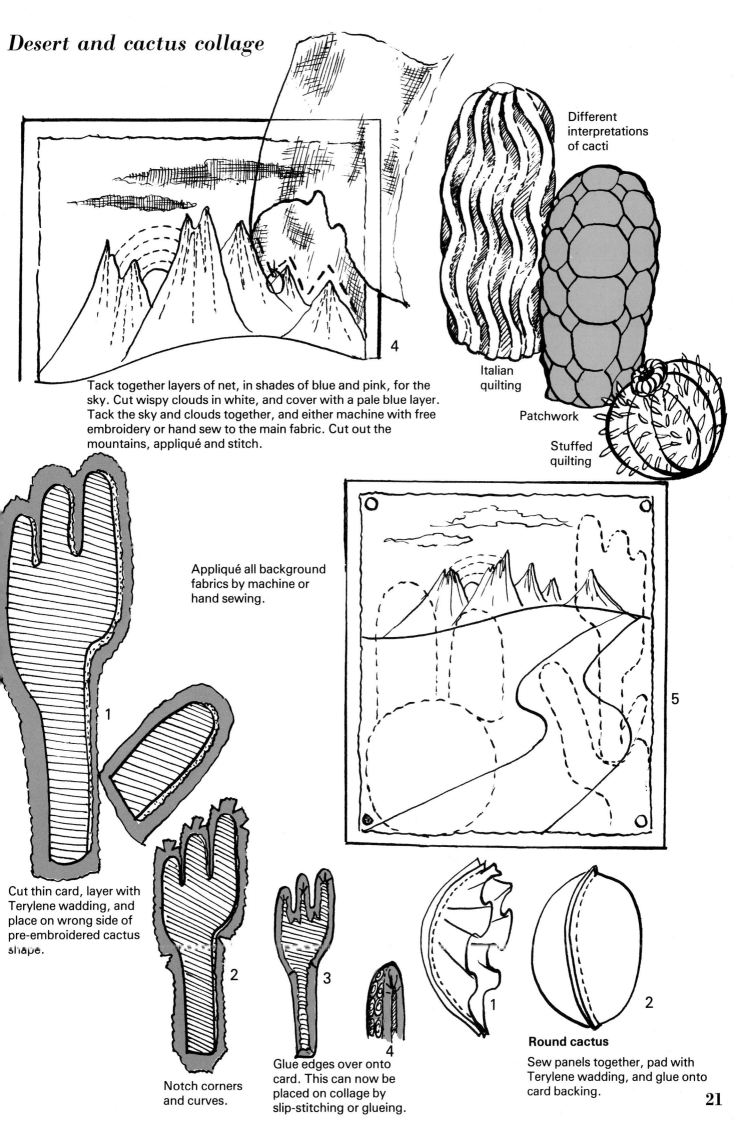

4

Tack together layers of net, in shades of blue and pink, for the sky. Cut wispy clouds in white, and cover with a pale blue layer. Tack the sky and clouds together, and either machine with free embroidery or hand sew to the main fabric. Cut out the mountains, appliqué and stitch.

Different interpretations of cacti

Italian quilting

Patchwork

Stuffed quilting

Appliqué all background fabrics by machine or hand sewing.

5

1

Cut thin card, layer with Terylene wadding, and place on wrong side of pre-embroidered cactus shape.

2   **3**   **4**

Notch corners and curves.

Glue edges over onto card. This can now be placed on collage by slip-stitching or glueing.

1   **2**

Round cactus

Sew panels together, pad with Terylene wadding, and glue onto card backing.

21

Desert and cactus collage

Finished collage, mounted on board (a simple wooden frame can be added)

Double knot stitch

Cactus using wide-ribbed needlecord, with thick tapestry-wool stitches

Crochet flowers in orange and yellow shades, in Perle thread.

Clamshell patchwork cactus with fan blanket stitch and French knots

Round cactus in quilted velvet, with buttonhole rings and beads

Cactus on satin ground, using Perle thread, cable and backstitch

Mounting work for framing

All work should be stretched first to remove creases and distortion. Cut card to size of picture. Trim collage, allowing 6 cm all round for hem.

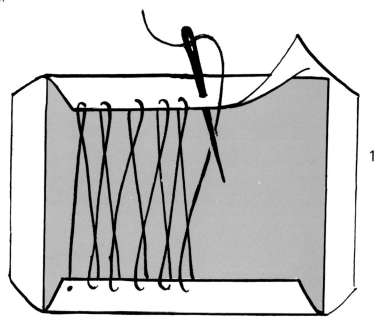

Lace fabric across card, pulling firmly on grain.

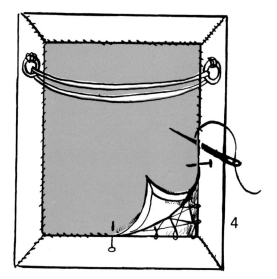

Mitre corners and attach two curtain rings, one on either side.

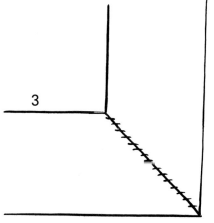

Sew on backing fabric. Loop picture cord through rings. The picture can be hung unframed, or is now ready to be put in a simple frame.

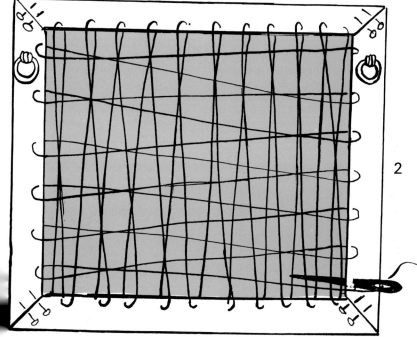

Oversew mitred corners.

The kitchen as a source of inspiration

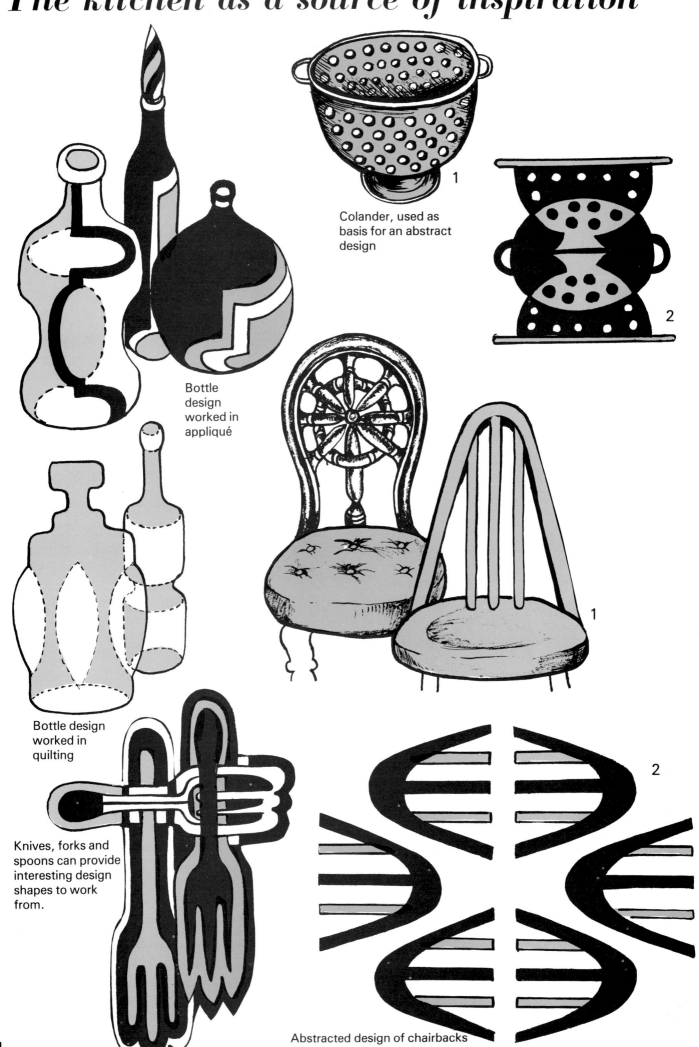

Colander, used as basis for an abstract design

1

2

Bottle design worked in appliqué

Bottle design worked in quilting

1

2

Knives, forks and spoons can provide interesting design shapes to work from.

Abstracted design of chairbacks

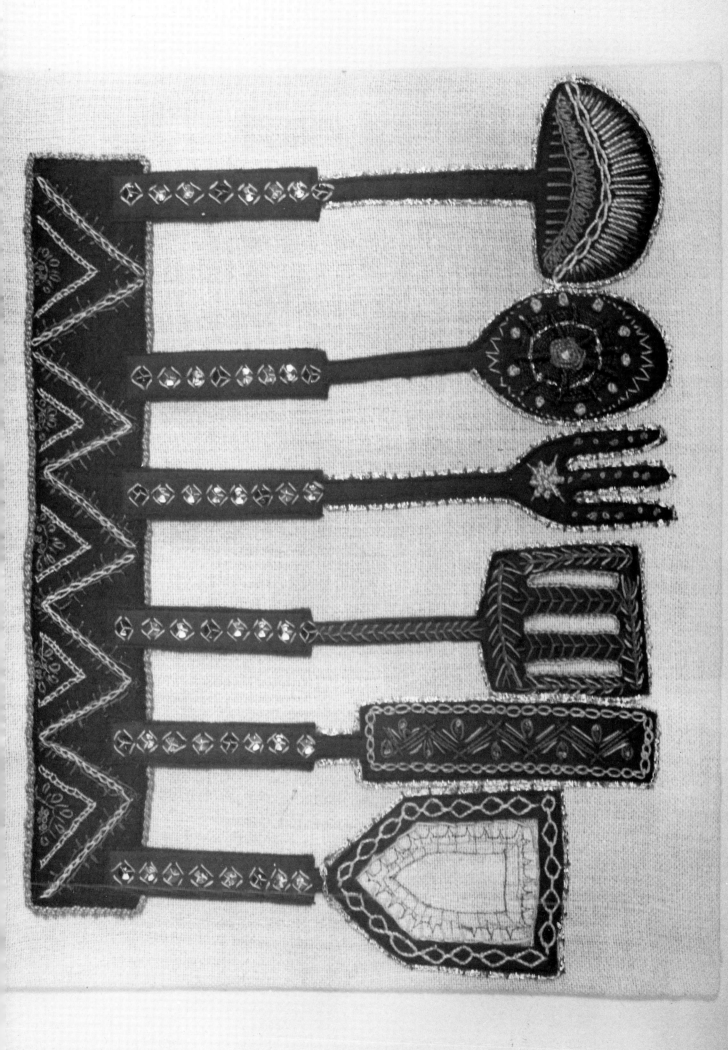

Lampshade in shadow-work

Worked organdie or net, or any other transparent fabric, with the bulk of the design worked on the wrong side in a closed herringbone stitch, producing areas of shaded colour on the right side. A limited number of surface stitches can be introduced, remembering that the back and front must be neatly finished, with no extra threads joining from stitch to stitch.

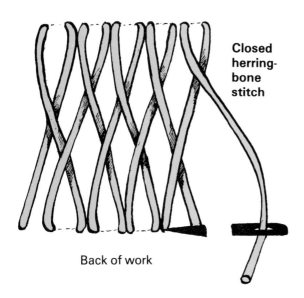

Closed herring-bone stitch

Back of work

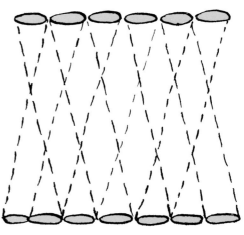

Front of work: the stitches at the back show through the organdie as a fine shadow-work. Stitches can be worked in self or contrasting shades, in a single stranded thread.

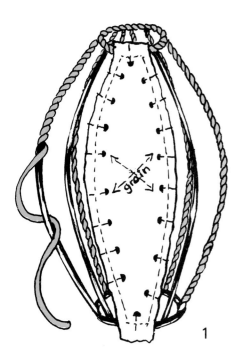

The wires are bound with plain cotton tape. The pattern for the panels is obtained by pinning the fabric to the wires. Cut on the cross-grain of the fabric.

1

Design motif in closed herringbone, satin and chain stitch and French knots

2

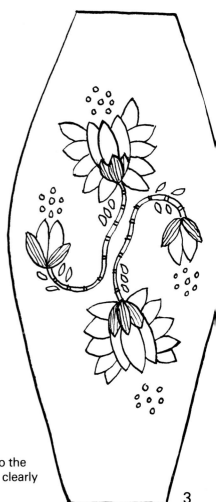

Design motif incorporated into the shape of the panel and drawn clearly on firm paper

3

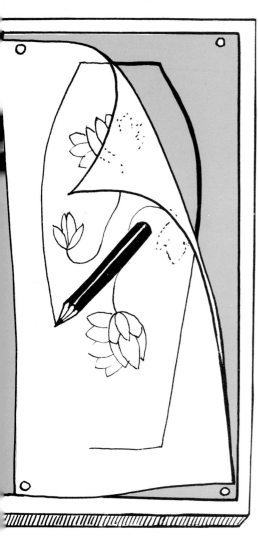

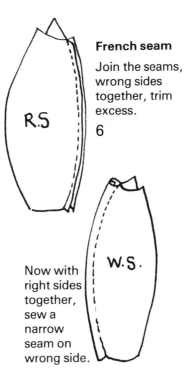

French seam

Join the seams, wrong sides together, trim excess.

6

Now with right sides together, sew a narrow seam on wrong side.

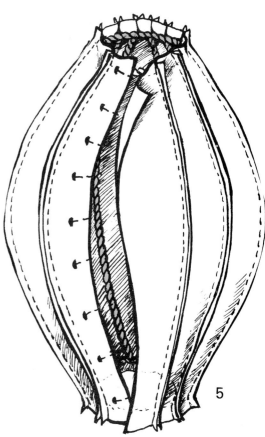

5

Pin the panels loosely on the frame, to get correct fit. Finish with a French seam (this will draw the fabric taut on the frame). The final seam is turned under and slip-stitched to the binding on the wire.

4

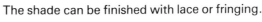

Place organdie over design, draw the shapes through with a fine pencil, and trace in the stitch lines. Repeat for all the panels needed for the lampshade.

7

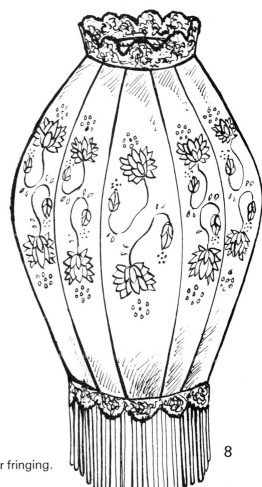

8

The shade can be finished with lace or fringing.

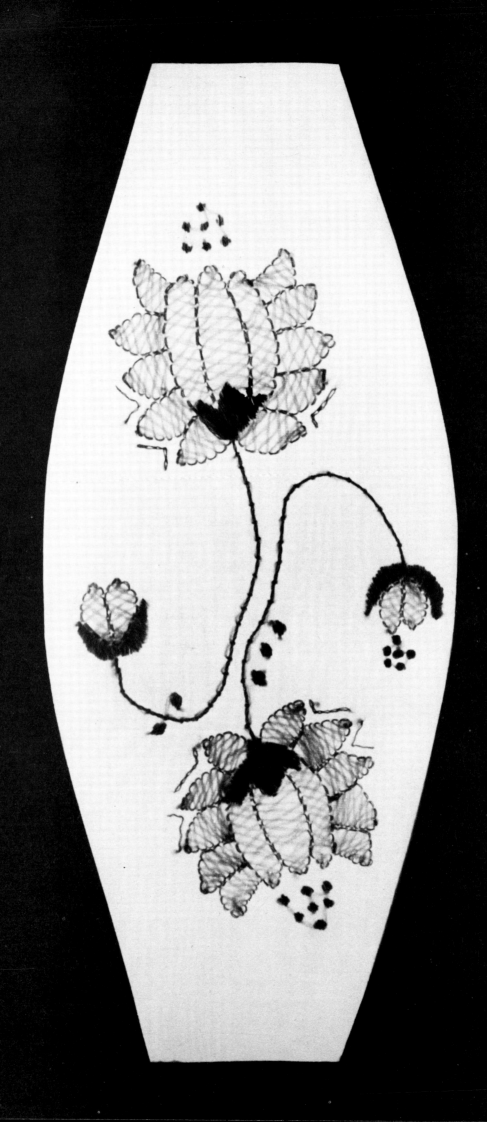

Cords and fringes

Cords

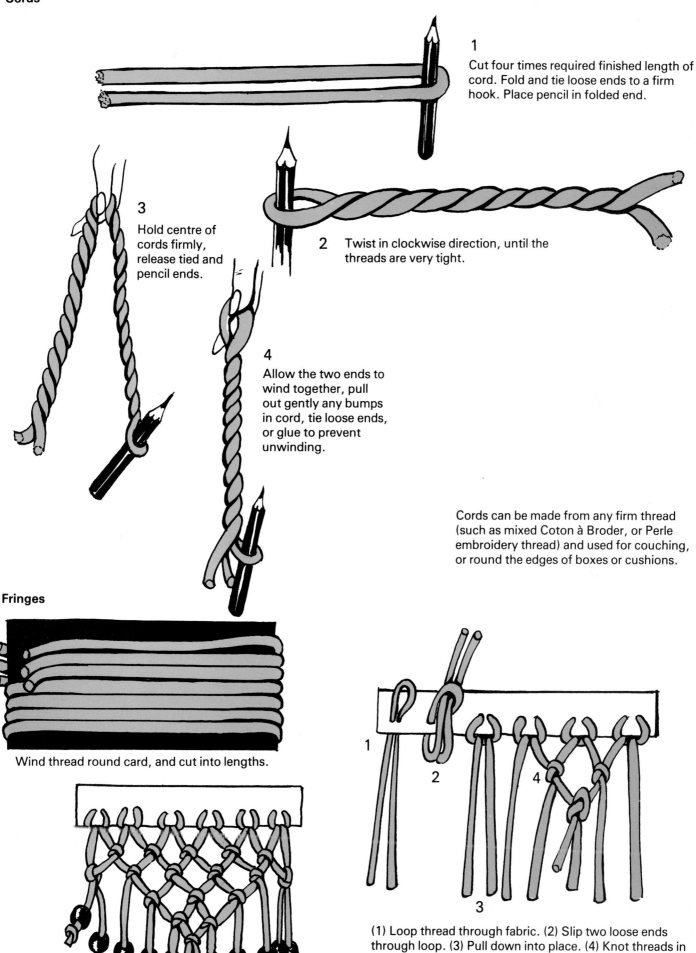

1

Cut four times required finished length of cord. Fold and tie loose ends to a firm hook. Place pencil in folded end.

2

Twist in clockwise direction, until the threads are very tight.

3

Hold centre of cords firmly, release tied and pencil ends.

4

Allow the two ends to wind together, pull out gently any bumps in cord, tie loose ends, or glue to prevent unwinding.

Cords can be made from any firm thread (such as mixed Coton à Broder, or Perle embroidery thread) and used for couching, or round the edges of boxes or cushions.

Fringes

Wind thread round card, and cut into lengths.

(1) Loop thread through fabric. (2) Slip two loose ends through loop. (3) Pull down into place. (4) Knot threads in alternate rows.

Fringing can be knotted into various shapes and designs, and can also be finished off with beading.

Bird collage

Use birds as a source of inspiration: these can be incorporated into a background. Draw birds carefully from life or photographs.

Draw a suitable background: here we have a lakeside, with distant trees and cloud formations and a foreground of heavy fencing.

Trace the design and prepare the background. Tack the birds' outlines in position.

The whole background can then be machined or hand sewn. Use layers of net for water, clouds and sky, with textured tweed for the shoreline. The heavy fencing can be made in padded suede or leather.

Lakeside, with birds arranged and drawn in to form collage design.

Prepared background with final positions of birds indicated

Bird collage

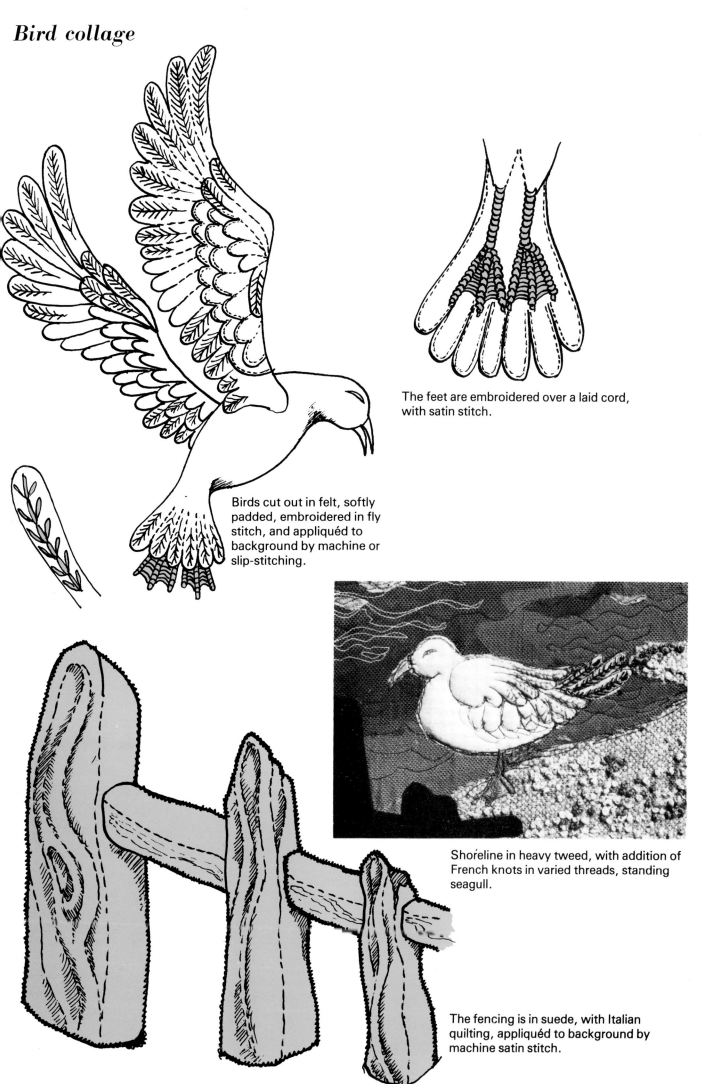

The feet are embroidered over a laid cord, with satin stitch.

Birds cut out in felt, softly padded, embroidered in fly stitch, and appliquéd to background by machine or slip-stitching.

Shoreline in heavy tweed, with addition of French knots in varied threads, standing seagull.

The fencing is in suede, with Italian quilting, appliquéd to background by machine satin stitch.